WHAT'S YOUR VIEW?

KEEPING PEACE IN THE WORLD

Adam Hibbert

A+

Smart Apple Media

First published in 2006 by Franklin Watts
338 Euston Road, London NW1 3BH

Franklin Watts Australia, Hachette Children's Books
Level 17/207 Kent Street, Sydney NSW 2000

Series editor: Sarah Peutrill, **Art director:** Jonathan Hair, **Design:** Proof Books,
Picture researcher: Sophie Hartley

Picture and text credits: see page 48.

Note on Web sites:
Every effort has been made by the publishers to ensure that the Web sites in this book
contain no inappropriate or offensive material. However, because of the nature of the
Internet, it is impossible to guarantee that the contents of these sites will not be altered.
We strongly advise that Internet access be supervised by a responsible adult.

Published in the United States by Smart Apple Media
2140 Howard Drive West, North Mankato, Minnesota 56003

Library of Congress Cataloging-in-Publication Data

Hibbert, Adam, 1968-
Keeping peace in the world / by Adam Hibbert.
p. cm. — (What's your view?)
ISBN-13: 978-1-58340-971-8
1. Peace-building. 2. United Nations. I. Title. II. Series.

JZ5538.H53 2006
327.1'72—dc22   2005037712

9 8 7 6 5 4 3 2 1

Contents

4 What's the issue?

6 Is it my country's duty to intervene in other people's wars?

8 Does European integration improve hopes for world peace?

10 Can sanctions help people in the sanctioned country?

12 Does the UN Security Council work?

14 Do crimes against humanity justify invading a country?

16 Is "preemptive" war making the world safer?

18 Does UN peacekeeping work?

20 Could 1994's massacres in Rwanda have been prevented?

22 Do controls on the arms trade help peace?

24 Was NATO's 1999 Kosovo War justified?

26 Does terrorism ever make sense?

28 Should Amnesty International support attacks on "rogue" regimes?

30 Is ethnic hatred the world's biggest threat to peace?

32 Does the UN act independently of U.S. interests?

34 Will environmental crises lead to wars?

36 Should alleged human rights criminals be tried in an international court?

38 Can the Palestinian–Israeli conflict be solved by peace talks?

40 Will laws against land mines work?

42 Is it possible to win a war against terror?

44 Glossary

46 Debating tips

47 Index

48 Acknowledgements

What's the issue?

PEACE IS not as easy to achieve as most of us wish. In a world of competing nations and groups, it takes hard work to maintain peace. The horror and chaos of World War II (1939–1945) made its survivors determined to protect peace. They founded the United Nations (UN) in 1945 to help nations solve their disagreements peaceably and oversee a more law-abiding and democratic community of nations.

Cold War (1945–1990)

In 1945, two rival superpowers, the United States and the Union of Soviet Socialist Republics (USSR)—which included Russia and 14 other Soviet republics—dominated the world the UN faced. Both superpowers had a vote on the UN Security Council, the organization's top decision-making body. Each used its vote to stop the other from exploiting the UN. Until the USSR collapsed around 1990, this balance within the UN had the effect of limiting its activities to a few urgent humanitarian tasks.

The UN operation in Cyprus is one of its longest-running peace projects, begun in 1964. UN peacekeepers patrol a "peace line" between northern (Turkish) Cyprus and southern (Greek) Cyprus, set up during a ceasefire in 1974. The UN made a new attempt to unite the two sides in 2004. It failed, and the peace line remained, still dividing the capital city of Nicosia (pictured).

New world order (1991–present)

The collapse of the USSR upset the global balance. The U.S. was suddenly the world's only superpower. New powers emerged, such as the European Union (EU) and a group of developing world nations led by China, India, and Brazil. To prevent dangerous instability, the U.S. recommended a new "vision" for a community of nations, united under its leadership. President George H. Bush described this vision as "a new world order."

> "This is an historic moment. We have in this past year made great progress in ending the long era of conflict and cold war. We have before us the opportunity to forge for ourselves and for future generations a new world order, a world where the rule of law, not the law of the jungle, governs the conduct of nations. When we are successful, and we will be, we have a real chance at this new world order, an order in which a credible United Nations can use its peacekeeping role to fulfill the promise and vision of the UN's founders."

President George H. Bush, announcing the start of the 1991 Gulf War

From peacekeeping to peacemaking?

After the USSR collapsed, other governments that depended on it for support grew unstable, and civil wars broke out. The UN became a more active "world police force." But it still relied on its 1945 principles, acting only with the agreement of those involved in a dispute. The U.S. and others wanted to take peacekeeping further. Instead of just policing agreed ceasefires, they wanted the UN to allow armed "humanitarian interventions" to stop conflicts, against the wishes of those involved. This policy disagreement, between peacekeeping and military humanitarian interventions, caused a crisis in 1999 over the Kosovo War (see page 24). It has divided the UN ever since.

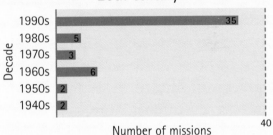

Number of UN peacekeeping missions, 20th century

Case studies—countries

Countries that are particular conflict areas are mentioned throughout the book in various quotes. To find out more about the background to these conflicts, see the country case studies:

Bosnia: p. 9
Chile: p. 36
China: p. 14
Iraq: p. 16
Israel: pp. 38–39
Kosovo: p. 25
Kurdistan: p. 30
Lesotho: p. 35
Liberia: pp. 7 and 19
Rwanda: p. 21
South Africa: pp. 10 and 27

Note on quotes

Quotes presented in this book in a specific context should not be understood to commit their source to one side of that debate. They are simply illustrations of the possible viewpoints in each debate.

Q: Is it my country's duty to intervene in other people's wars?

WHEN WE see images of conflict in another country, most of us wish there was something we could do to ease the suffering. Nongovernmental organizations (NGOs), such as charities and the International Committee of the Red Cross (ICRC), can pass aid quickly to suffering people. Many people also believe that our governments should use resources they control, such as military personnel and aircraft, to help. Some also argue that our governments should send soldiers into conflicts to forcibly stop the fighting.

✳ STATISTICALLY SPEAKING

"My country should contribute troops to Iraq"

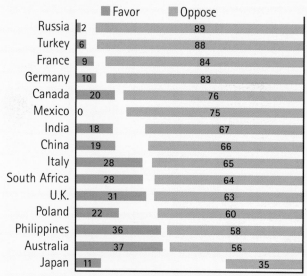

■ Favor ▨ Oppose

Country	Favor	Oppose
Russia	2	89
Turkey	6	88
France	9	84
Germany	10	83
Canada	20	76
Mexico	0	75
India	18	67
China	19	66
Italy	28	65
South Africa	28	64
U.K.	31	63
Poland	22	60
Philippines	36	58
Australia	37	56
Japan	11	35

The spaces between the bars show "depends" or "neither."

Source: BBC World Service poll (February 2005)

YES

"We must pursue justice, help the suffering, and overthrow tyrants. But there are limits to our power. We must pick our tyrants carefully, keeping in mind not only justice but our practical interests and the worldwide consequences of what we intend. Our duty in this area is like our obligation to show charity. We have no power to help everyone and no right to help no one."

David Gelernter, columnist, U.S.

✓ "As a permanent member of the UN Security Council [see page 12] and as a country both willing and able to play a leading role internationally, we have a responsibility to act as a force for good in the world."

United Kingdom (U.K.) government, Strategic Defense Review

✓ "The reluctance of the United States to commit to a force of willing countries under the banner of the United Nations to stop the bloodshed in East Timor points to a lack of interest in the [Australian] region and a disregard for its long-standing relationship with Australia. If America decides not to participate, it would have failed its ally, the region, and the cause of democracy."

Editorial on East Timor, The Sydney Daily Telegraph, Australia

CASE STUDY

ECOMOG

West African nations created an army, ECOMOG, to stop the Liberian civil war of 1990–1998 (see page 19). ECOMOG lacked experience and suffered serious casualties, but it may have helped to end the civil war. It has also taken action in Sierra Leone and Guinea-Bissau. A few people refuse to accept ECOMOG as a peacekeeping force, claiming that it is a tool mainly for Nigeria's own purposes.

The war in figures

Of a population of 2.8 million Liberians before the war:

- 200,000 total killed
- 700,000 refugees
- 1.4 million internally displaced
- 33,000 combatants survived
- 20,322 combatants disarmed

Charles Taylor (pictured) began Liberia's civil war but lost control of his allies. Liberia was devastated by fighting between seven warlords.

NO

"America . . . does not go abroad in search of monsters to destroy. She is well-wisher to the freedom and independence of all. She is the champion and vindicator only of her own."

John Quincy Adams, U.S. Secretary of State (1821)

✗ "Foreign intervention is unjustified in any way. In the first place, who gave the interventionists the right to intervene? What is the basis on which they are intervening? Such actions create more problems rather than find a solution."

Kweku Mamuah, Africa, BBC Online "Talking Point"

✗ "The United States should respond to Colombia's challenge with diplomatic support, social and economic help. . . . We should not intervene on one side of another country's civil war."

Robert E. White, President of the U.S. Center for International Policy and former U.S. Ambassador to Paraguay and El Salvador

MORE TO THINK ABOUT

Civil wars occur when groups within a society lose the ability to reach political compromises. Compare the effort to force two warring factions back together with forcing a divorced couple to remarry. What does the comparison suggest to you?

FIND OUT MORE: www.ecowas.int www.swisspeace.org/fast
www.crisisweb.org www.cryfreetown.org

Q: Does European integration improve hopes for world peace?

WORLD WAR I (1914–1918) and World War II (1939–1945) both started within Europe. Rivalry between the most powerful European nations—Germany, France, Russia, Britain, and Italy—was once the main source of instability in the world. For this reason, some see the cooperation of Germany, France, Britain, Italy, and others in the European Union as a step toward enduring peace. Others see the growing strength of the EU as a threat to the "world order" led by the U.S.

YES

"I think [the enlarged EU] will be a success, for a simple reason: it represents progress, progress in building the peaceful and democratic Europe, and a Europe that is going to facilitate economic developments and social progress."

Jacques Chirac, President of France

"The Treaty on the Constitution for Europe [establishes] a kind of peaceful, democratic 'empire'—both for its citizens and for the rest of the world."

Dusko Lopandic, Serbian European Integration Office

✺ STATISTICALLY SPEAKING

Swedish citizens favor EU military:
- 60 percent oppose involvement in the North Atlantic Treaty Organization (NATO)
- 62 percent support an EU armed force

NO

"U.S.-EU competition will extend far beyond the realm of trade. The U.S. Federal Reserve and the European Central Bank are destined to vie for control of the international monetary system. . . . An ascendant EU will surely test its muscle against America. . . . A once-united West appears well on its way to separating into competing halves."

Charles A. Kupchan, "The End of The West," in The Atlantic

"Whatever its origin, Europe today is no longer just about peace. It is about projecting collective power. That is one very clear reason . . . why the central European nations want to join."

Tony Blair, U.K. Prime Minister, in a speech to the Polish Stock Exchange

"[Congress] deplores the recent increase in arms sales by member states of the European Union to . . . China, . . . actions that place European security policy in direct conflict with United States security interests."

U.S. House of Representatives Resolution 57

BOSNIA

On March 18, 1992, leaders of the Serbs, Croats, and Muslim ethnic groups of Bosnia met in Sarajevo to agree to an EU-sponsored plan to divide Bosnia peacefully into ethnic regions. The plan failed, and war broke out. At first, Croats and Muslims worked together to fight Serbs, who had the most powerful army. Then, in 1993, Croats and Muslims began to fight each other as well. Between 100,000 and 250,000 people died, and more than 1 million became refugees. The war finally ended under a U.S.-sponsored plan, the Dayton Agreement, at the end of 1995. Like the peace plan before the war, it divided Bosnia into ethnic territories.

(Left to right) Bosnian President Alija Izetbegovic, Serbian President Slobodan Milosevic, and French President Jacques Chirac met in Paris in 1996. They discussed how to heal the deep divisions left over from the war. Earlier EU attempts to keep the opposing sides talking failed to prevent the war.

✳ STATISTICALLY SPEAKING

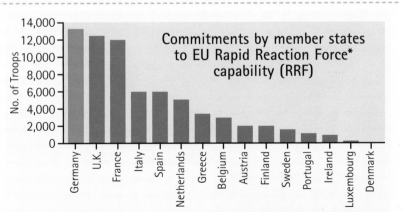

Commitments by member states to EU Rapid Reaction Force* capability (RRF)

No. of Troops

*A Rapid Reaction Force is a military unit designed to respond in very short time frames to emergencies—for example, within hours or days.

Source: www.europeanmovement.ie

MORE TO THINK ABOUT

A stronger EU makes war between major European nations less likely. But if that stronger "bloc" of countries is seen as a rival by another world power, might a new "cold war" develop? Find out what a "proxy war" is.

Q: Can sanctions help people in the sanctioned country?

IF A COUNTRY ignores requests from other countries to change its policies, one option for the international community is to "sanction" the country—to withdraw trade and cultural links. This causes economic problems for any country, but especially for those with small economies. This can make the country's government unpopular with its own citizens, forcing it to think again. But sanctions might also cause greater hardship for poor people.

CASE STUDY

SANCTIONS IN SOUTH AFRICA

The white South African government was sanctioned in 1977, after it murdered black rights activist Steve Biko. The sanctions aimed to deny the racist government access to weapons. But South Africa responded by enlarging its own arms industry. By the mid-1980s, the UN needed new sanctions to block the export of South Africa's surplus arms.

Arms industry employees, South Africa

Before 1977 sanctions by UN	less than 10,000
During sanctions	120,000

Black South Africans were banned from politics and voting. These protesters in 1986 risked harsh treatment by the regime's security forces.

NO "In the 1990s, trade sanctions imposed on Yugoslavia enriched a criminal elite closely tied to paramilitary organizations and arch-nationalist political parties. The loosely enforced blockade on gasoline produced an extremely profitable black market controlled by these criminals."

Stanley Weiss & Zachary Selden, "Often Worse than Ineffective," in UN Chronicle

✗ "Sanctions inevitably affect the lives of ordinary citizens in the targeted states; indeed, they are basically the 20th century's equivalent of the long and cruel sieges of cities during the Middle Ages."

Michel Rossignol, author of "Sanctions"

✗ "We are in danger of losing the argument or propaganda war—if we haven't lost it already—about who is responsible for this situation, President Saddam Hussein or the UN. . . . We are accused of causing suffering to an entire population."

Kofi Annan, UN Secretary-General, speaking about sanctions on Iraq

YES "The economic sanctions you imposed . . . have brought us to the point where the transition to democracy has now been enshrined in the law of our country."

Nelson Mandela, first President of South Africa after apartheid ended

✓ "By denying aggressors and human rights abusers the implements of war and repression, arms embargoes contribute directly to preventing and reducing the level of armed conflict."

David Cortright & George Lopez, The Sanctions Decade

✓ "Sanctions have met with success in more than a few instances. . . . Financial sanctions can be particularly effective. . . . [Making capital more expensive] hurts the elite of the target country, who then have to make some hard choices."

Stanley Weiss & Zachary Selden, "Often Worse than Ineffective," in UN Chronicle

✹ STATISTICALLY SPEAKING

Impact of sanctions on Iraq

Measure	Before	During
GDP* per person	$2,840 (1989)	$200 (1997)
Birth rate	40.3/1,000 (1985–90)	38.4/1,000 (1990–95)
Death rate	7.2/1,000 (1985–90)	10.4/1,000 (1990–95)
Under-5 death rate	56 per 1,000	131 per 1,000
Under-1 death rate	47 per 1,000	108 per 1,000

* GDP = Gross Domestic Product, a measure of a country's wealth

Source: www.merip.org

MORE TO THINK ABOUT

Sanctions are a peaceful way to discipline a country that is causing concern. But they are not painless for either side. Poor people suffer in the target country, and the sanctioning countries may lose business and jobs. In what circumstances do you think this is justified?

Q: Does the UN Security Council work?

The UN Security Council (UNSC) is the body that makes the UN's peacekeeping decisions. Five of the "seats" in the council are held by permanent members—China, France, Russia, the U.K., and the U.S. The other 10 seats are held for 2-year periods by countries elected by the General Assembly of UN member nations. Decisions need the support of at least nine members. The five permanent members, or "P-5," each have a special "negative" vote, called a veto, which they can use to overrule the majority. The Security Council can impose peaceful sanctions on a country. In extreme cases, it authorizes member nations to intervene with military force.

The invasion of Iraq in 2003 was denied permission by the UN Security Council. Weapons inspector Hans Blix (pictured) was one of the leading figures in the debate. According to a UN spokesperson at the time, "The Security Council has seldom functioned better than in recent months, when it has been the scene of vigorous discussion."

YES

"Time and time again, this flawed organization becomes essential for us, and when we work with it and with the key countries in it, we can achieve a great deal."
Richard Holbrooke, U.S. diplomat

"Imagine the world without the UN. It would be anarchy."
Dysane Dorani, UN information director

"I am a proud internationalist. To paraphrase Winston Churchill, for all its flaws, the United Nations, of all the options, is the least worst international governing body invented so far."
Senator John Cherry, speech to the Australian Parliament

CASE STUDY

THE SECURITY COUNCIL'S VETO

The veto of the five permanent members of the security council can be used to overrule the majority.

"[Permanent Members] claim that . . . they have been much more responsible in the use of the veto. However, . . . it is the *threat* of the use of the veto that . . . has led to a series of steps that are completely undesirable, undemocratic, and subversive of the UN:

• Forcing the UN to discontinue action (Somalia)
• Preventing action (Rwanda)
• Forcing action of interest only to a permanent member
• Permitting completely illegal action (Iraq no-fly zones)
• Completely marginalizing the UN (Kosovo)."

Source: Satyabrata Pal, "Statement to the OEWG on Security Council Reform"

NO "In Rwanda, in the face of full-scale genocide, the Security Council . . . refused to act, a shameful decision insisted upon by the United States. And in the later 1990s, the Security Council failed to act to enforce its own resolutions regarding Iraq, thereby leaving in place a great menace to world peace."

Joshua Muravchik, in "Enhancing U.S. Leadership at the UN"

✖ "The UN . . . has made mistakes that are so grave [in East Timor] that they border on criminal irresponsibility."

Guy Taillerfer, Canada's Le Devoir

✖ "Looking to the UN to protect individuals . . . from abuses of government power makes as much sense as looking to the International Tobacco Growers' Association to protect individuals from the dangers of smoking."

Carroll Andrew Morse, "The UN: The World's Greatest Trade Association"

✴ STATISTICALLY SPEAKING

• Security Council resolutions breached

Iraq 16	Israel 29

Source: "UN's 'Two Standards' Under Fire," www.csmonitor.com

✴ STATISTICALLY SPEAKING

Vetoes cast by UN Security Council members

Years	China	U.K.	France	U.S.	Russia
1946–55	(1*)	0	2	0	80
1956–65	0	3	2	0	26
1966–75	2	10	2	12	7
1976–85	0	11	9	34	6
1986–95	0	8	3	24	2
1996–2004	2	0	0	10	1
Total	4(5*)	32	18	80	122

*(*Includes vote cast by Taiwan in 1955 while occupying China's seat)*

Source: www.globalpolicy.org

MORE TO THINK ABOUT

Some people see the UN Security Council as flawed—but representative of the real world in which countries are not truly equal. Do you think the veto power of the P–5 should be removed? What would that do, for example, to U.S. support for the UN?

FIND OUT MORE: www.csmonitor.com www.osce.org www.un.int/india/ind103.htm
www.people.howstuffworks.com/united-nations.htm

Q: Do crimes against humanity justify invading a country?

LAWS FORBIDDING "crimes against humanity" began to be created in 1945 to deter political leaders from inhumane behavior. Suspects can be brought to trial by the international community. But invading a country to stop a government's ongoing abuse is much more challenging. It forces the UN to overrule the right of its own members to be independent, known as their "sovereignty."

CASE STUDY

CHINA AND TIANANMEN SQUARE

In 1989, a large demonstration in Beijing, China, was broken up by the Chinese army. In the confrontations that followed, many hundreds of people were killed, and thousands were injured and imprisoned. UN members accused the Chinese government of abusing the protesters' human rights. China disagreed, and no action was taken against it.

Tiananmen protesters were demanding more democracy and less government corruption. News of their mistreatment angered the international community.

✿ STATISTICALLY SPEAKING

Did NATO's Kosovo intervention (see pages 24–25) achieve its humanitarian goal?

	Refugees' ethnic identity	Number of refugees
Before NATO bombing	Albanian	250,000–300,000
During NATO bombing	Albanian, Serb, Roma	900,000–1,200,000
After NATO bombing	Serb, Roma	220,000–280,000

Source: www.unhcr.org

YES

"I think there is a lot to be learned by the international community. I don't see them learning any lessons, given what has been happening in my country since the days the genocide was being planned and prepared and nothing was done to stop that, and there was a presence of the international community on the ground—they were seeing all that happen."

President Paul Kagame of Rwanda

✔ "The freedom to be left alone is vital, but it is ultimately more suited to bears than to human beings."

Gary Kamiya, "The Strange Rise of Libertarianism"

✔ "The ultimate goal of the human rights movement . . . is not . . . peace and stability, but to promote and protect human rights. . . . This means that states may have to be ready to risk a certain deterioration of interstate relations."

Rein Müllerson, Human Rights Diplomacy

NO

"Didn't colonial powers entering Africa toward the end of the 19th century claim to be stamping out slavery? . . . Hasn't every imperial intervention claimed to be humanitarian?"

Mahmood Mamdani, in "Humanitarian Intervention: A Forum," in The Nation

✘ "In 1938, Hitler used the grievances of ethnic Germans to justify his seizure of the Sudetenland from Czechoslovakia."

John T. Correll, "The Doctrine of Intervention," in Air Force Magazine

✘ "Even in autocratic states, the will of the people is a force that cannot be ignored indefinitely—as the demise of many autocratic regimes over the decades has shown. America is a democracy, but it is not accountable to the people of Afghanistan—it acts on the basis of the will of the American people, and the will of the Afghan people is not even known."

Jon Holbrook, "In Defense of Sovereignty"

MORE TO THINK ABOUT
Crimes against humanity include a range of human rights abuses. If the UN's most powerful members are guilty of such abuses, as many people believe, how could the UN stop them?

Q: Is "preemptive" war making the world safer?

In 2001, after the 9/11 terrorist attacks, the U.S. and its allies began to talk about a "war on terror"—against countries thought to pose danger. In 2003, a U.S.-led coalition invaded Iraq, one of the "threatening" countries. UN law forbids nations from starting a war, with one exception—when starting a war is the nation's best chance to defend itself from an immediate threat. But could this type of "preemptive" war be an excuse for wars of aggression?

YES

"The war on terror will not be won on the defensive. We must take the battle to the enemy, disrupt his plans, and confront the worst threats before they emerge. In the world we have entered, the only path to safety is the path of action. And this nation will act."

George W. Bush, speech to graduates of West Point Military Academy

"Far from being a distraction, the preemptive war against Saddam Hussein has enhanced the ability of the United States to deter North Korea from its sinister plans."

David Horowitz, www.frontpagemagazine.com

CASE STUDY 1

IRAQ

Formerly part of the Turkish Ottoman Empire, Iraq became a "republic" in 1958, but a series of dictators ruled the country—the latest was Saddam Hussein. Territorial disputes with neighboring Iran led to an eight-year war (1980–88). In August 1990, Iraq invaded Kuwait, but a coalition of forces freed Kuwait in 1991. Following this, the UN Security Council demanded that Iraq scrap its weapons of mass destruction and allow weapons inspections. Continued Iraqi non-compliance for 12 years resulted in the U.S.-led invasion of Iraq in 2003. Saddam Hussein was seized and lost control of Iraq. Coalition forces struggled to restore degraded infrastructure and establish a new government.

NO

"When you accuse another nation of breaking the rules, you do so by the rules. You cannot be a self-appointed world policeman or deputy sheriff and engage in a bit of vigilante international justice on the side."

Senator John Cherry, speech to the Australian Parliament

"You don't 'prevent' anything by war . . . except peace."

President Harry S. Truman, cited by Senator Edward Kennedy, opposing the 2003 Iraq war

"By relying on force alone, the U.S. government has sacrificed one of its major weapons in the struggle against terrorism; namely, its own reputation as an exemplar of human rights."

William F. Schulz, Amnesty International press conference

CASE STUDY 2

SIX-DAY WAR

On June 5, 1967, Israel launched a preemptive air war against its neighbors. It caught the Egyptian Air Force by surprise and totally disabled its fleet of planes. The Six-Day War was seen as Israel's only chance to defend itself against an invasion being organized by Egypt, Jordan, and Syria. Israel's victory secured peace with its neighbors from that time on.

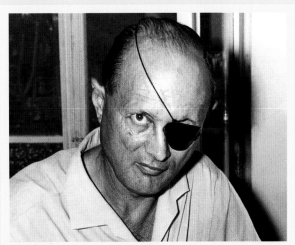

Moshe Dayan, Israel's defense minister in 1967, became a national hero for his successful preemptive strike.

✹ STATISTICALLY SPEAKING

Have U.S. [preemptive] actions in Iraq made the world safer?

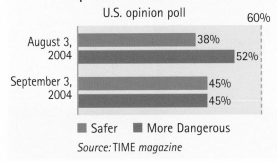

U.S. opinion poll

August 3, 2004	38% / 52%
September 3, 2004	45% / 45%

60%

■ Safer   ■ More Dangerous

Source: TIME magazine

What effect has the Iraq war had on the war on terror? (Figures in %)

Country	Helped	Hurt	No effect	Don't know
U.S.	62	28	3	7
U.K.	36	50	5	9
France	33	55	10	2
Germany	30	58	5	7
Russia	22	50	18	10
Turkey	24	56	8	12
Pakistan	8	57	6	29
Jordan	12	36	37	15
Morocco	16	67	8	9

Source: Pew Global Attitudes Survey, March 2004

MORE TO THINK ABOUT

Does the use of force set a bad example, or must rules be backed up by force?

Q: Does UN peacekeeping work?

UN PEACEKEEPERS keep warring peoples apart to establish peace and allow people to go back to their normal economic activities. In this sense, UN peacekeepers have saved tens of thousands of lives over the UN's first 50 years. But there are many weaknesses in the system. The complex nature of war—especially civil wars—makes it impossible for a UN intervention to "fix" a crisis. That is a political task that warring groups have to settle between themselves.

YES

"The UN forces represent the manifest will of the community of nations to achieve peace through negotiations, and the forces have, by their presence, made a decisive contribution toward the initiation of actual peace negotiations."

Nobel Committee, announcement of award of 1998 Nobel Peace Prize to UN peacekeeping forces

"One . . . estimate indicates that the risk of renewed fighting is almost 70 percent lower when a peace operation is present than when belligerents are left to their own devices. . . . Any way you slice the data, it is quite clear that peacekeeping has a substantial . . . positive effect on stability—peacekeeping works."

Page Fortna, "Peace Operations: Futile or Vital?"

Dutch UN peacekeepers patrol the 10-square-mile (25 sq km) Temporary Security Zone (TSZ) between Ethiopia and Eritrea.

NO

"UN territories like Kosovo are the global equivalent of inner-city public housing, with the blue helmets as local enforcers for the absentee slum landlord. By contrast, a couple of years after 'imperialist warmonger' Bush showed up, Afghanistan and Iraq have elections, presidents, and prime ministers."

Mark Steyn, "UN Forces—Just a Bunch of Thugs"

✖ "Staff shortages in certain areas [in the Department of Peacekeeping Operations] are plainly obvious. . . . It is clearly not enough to have 32 officers providing military planning and guidance to 27,000 troops in the field."

Report of the Panel on UN Peace Operations

✖ "For [Dutch peacekeeper] Marc Klaver, the [UN's Srebrenica] safe area was a humiliating joke. The Muslims refused to be disarmed and carried out raids into Serb territory at night."

David Rohde, "End Game: The Betrayal of Srebrenica"

❊ STATISTICALLY SPEAKING

The Price of Peace?

UN peacekeeping finances

Budget, July 1, 2004 to June 30, 2005	$3.87 billion
Total cost of operations, 1948 to June 30, 2004	$31.54 billion
Unpaid member debts to peacekeeping	$2.26 billion

Source: www.un.org

CASE STUDY

LIBERIA

In September 2003, the UN Security Council sent a peacekeeping force to Liberia to support a ceasefire between the government and rebels. After 10 years of civil war, Liberia's economy, farms, and mining businesses were in ruins, and many Liberians were driven to extremes to survive.

The UN Mission in Liberia (UNMIL) placed 15,000 troops and 1,000 international police officers between the 2 armed groups. By 2005, 28 UN military troops and 2 UN police officers had died. The UN encouraged armed individuals to hand in weapons and bullets by offering a financial reward. Refugees brought in guns from surrounding countries, such as Côte d'Ivoire, to claim the rewards. An uneasy peace was maintained.

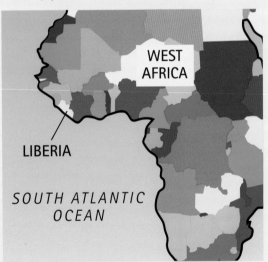

MORE TO THINK ABOUT

Peacekeeping may save lives in the area under control. But citizens of a country may object to it. Why do you think this is?

FIND OUT MORE: www.ipacademy.org www.nonviolentpeaceforce.org www.peaceoperations.org

Q: Could 1994's massacres in Rwanda have been prevented?

IN 1994, society broke down in the very poor African nation of Rwanda (see case study), leading to the deaths of approximately 650,000 civilians. As the world's media looked on in horror at the massacres, the international community appeared to do very little to prevent them.

NO

"The window of opportunity for [silencing genocide leaders] was within 48 hours of the initial killing. . . . It is hard to conceive of a government taking action to remove the leaders of another country in that . . . time."

Taylor B. Seybolt, "Could Genocide Have Been Stopped in Rwanda?"

✖ "By my calculations, three-quarters of the Tutsi victims would have died even if the West had launched a maximum intervention immediately."

Alan Kuperman, The Limits of Humanitarian Intervention

✖ "Coercive measures can cost lives and further divide communities and nations, without removing the tensions that first cause large-scale violence."

Quaker Council for European Affairs

YES

"The Force Commander of the United Nations Assistance Mission in Rwanda (UNAMIR) . . . still believes today that a force of 5,500 adequately trained and mechanized soldiers could have saved hundreds of thousands of lives."

Linda Melvern, "Humanitarian Intervention and the Case of Rwanda"

✔ "Since a battered collection of 500 UN peacekeepers managed to keep 25,000 Rwandans safe, a deployment of well-armed UN reinforcements, Pentagon radio jamming, or even mere moral attention from senior Washington policymakers might have saved many more. But we will never know."

Samantha Powers, investigative journalist

✔ "Had UNAMIR been reinforced several months prior to the outbreak of violence, as Belgium urged at the time, genocide might have been averted."

Alan Kuperman, "A Hard Look at Intervention"

❋ STATISTICALLY SPEAKING

Comparison of estimated lives saved before and during UN military intervention in Somalia

Somalian Civil War	Number who died	Number saved	Proportion saved
prior to UNOSOM I (Jan '91–Aug '92)	146,000–192,000	35,000–50,000	15.4–25.5%
UNOSOM I & OPR (Sept '92–Dec '92)	83,000–101,000	40,000	39.6–48.2%
UNITAF (Dec '92–May '93)	10,000–25,000	10,000	28.6–50%
UNOSOM II (May '93–Mar '95)	625–1,500	probably thousands	N/A

Source: Taylor B. Seybolt, "What Makes Humanitarian Military Interventions Effective?"

CASE STUDY

RWANDA

Rwanda has two main groups—the Hutu and the Tutsi. Wealthy Tutsi helped Belgium rule Rwanda from 1919 until Rwanda won independence in 1962. The Hutu majority took control, and up to 400,000 Tutsi fled to Uganda and elsewhere. With help from Uganda, the U.S., and the U.K., they created an army, the Rwandese Patriotic Front (RPF), in 1985. In 1990, the RPF invaded. In 1993, France and the U.S. oversaw a peace deal, the Arusha Accords. Moderate Hutu leaders accepted the deal, which gave the RPF significant power. Extreme Hutu politicians were excluded. To guarantee the deal, a small UN peacekeeping force and an RPF battalion were admitted to Rwanda's capital, Kigali.

CENTRAL AFRICA

SUDAN
ETHIOPIA
DEMOCRATIC REPUBLIC OF CONGO
UGANDA
KENYA
RWANDA
Lake Victoria
BURUNDI
INDIAN OCEAN
TANZANIA

But in April 1994, Rwanda's president was assassinated. Hutu extremists, fearing a Tutsi takeover, started killing moderate Hutu politicians, Tutsi leaders, and civilians. Ten Belgian UN troops were captured by extremist Hutu, tortured, and murdered. The UN evacuated 90 percent of its peace force. The killing stopped in July when the RPF conquered Kigali. By then, around 10 percent of the population was dead— between 600,000 and 1,000,000 people. Hundreds of thousands of Hutu fled to refugee camps, trying to escape Tutsi revenge attacks.

At Kibeho camp, up to 4,000 of 100,000 Hutu refugees were killed in revenge attacks by government troops in 1995.

MORE TO THINK ABOUT

The Tutsi rebel army made an official statement on April 30, 1994: "The Rwandese Patriotic Front hereby declares that it is categorically opposed to the proposed UN intervention force and will not . . . cooperate in its setting up and operation." Should the international community ignore such statements or take them into account when making a decision on whether to act?

FIND OUT MORE: www.h-net.org/~genocide www.facinghistory.org/
www.hrw.org www.globalpolicy.org

Q: Do controls on the arms trade help peace?

WARS CANNOT happen without weapons, so many UN programs and NGO campaigns try to limit the number of weapons available. Controls include limiting a country's arms exports, making international agreements to end the sale of arms to a particular customer, and spending money buying arms back to destroy them. Businesses that supply arms—and the governments that want to buy them—argue that this does not cure the causes of conflict.

A Sudanese Liberation Movement child soldier in West Dafur, Sudan, August 2004.

YES "By eliminating more than 51,000 items of treaty-limited equipment and conducting more than 2,400 on-site inspections, the 30 members of the treaty [the Conventional Armed Forces in Europe Treaty] have largely removed the threat of armed conflict in Europe."

John D. Holum, "Threat Control Through Arms Control"

✓ "Instead of contributing to recipient security, arms exports have contributed to political insecurity (e.g., Saudi Arabia) and sustained underdevelopment (e.g., South Africa)."

Campaign Against Arms Trade briefing

NO "The government's prime justification for supporting defense exports has always been to help maintain a strong defense industry that underpins our own security and to contribute to the security of friends and allies overseas."

Lord Bach, U.K. Minister of Defense Procurement

X "The fact that a shaky African state such as the Democratic Republic of Congo has 800,000 illegal guns doesn't mean that if the West were to tighten arms sales, the conflict would cease. People of the developing world are treated as children, with the idea that so long as dangerous implements are kept out of their reach, they won't cause any trouble."

Josie Appleton, "Jack Straw's Global Gun Law"

CONFLICTING EVIDENCE?

The value of global weapons transfer agreements (new deals made, not delivered and paid for) in 2003 was $25.3 billion—a sharp decline from 2000, when it stood at $40.3 billion.

Source: Congressional Research Service (CRS)

Ian Prichard, researcher for the Campaign Against the Arms Trade, said, "The CRS report on actual deliveries of arms—as opposed to arms agreements—showed no real downward trend was occurring."

Source: www.caat.org.uk

✳ STATISTICALLY SPEAKING

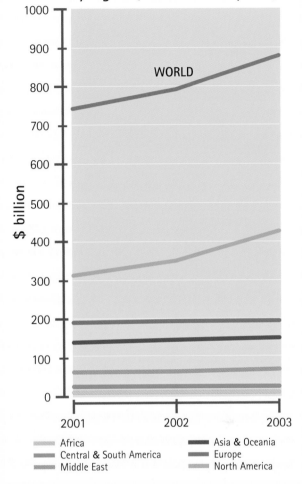

Military expenditures 2001–2003 by region (constant 2000 prices)

Legend:
- Africa
- Central & South America
- Middle East
- Asia & Oceania
- Europe
- North America

Source: SIPRI Yearbook 2004

Q: Was NATO's 1999 Kosovo War justified?

THE NORTH Atlantic Treaty Organization was established during the Cold War to help the U.S. organize Europe's defenses against the USSR. After the USSR's collapse around 1990, NATO came to be seen as a force that could actively police security problems. In 1999, without UN approval, NATO countries intervened in Kosovo, a province of Serbia where civil war was causing a humanitarian crisis (see case study).

British troops hold back Albanian demonstrators in Kosovo, 2000.

YES

"This [force] is the only way the international community can stop the genocide in Kosovo."
Jamie Shea, NATO spokesperson

"We are in no doubt that NATO is acting within international law."
George Robertson, prior to becoming NATO Secretary General

"All the evidence that was turned up by investigators, the UN, war crimes tribunals, journalists, showed that we had acted to prevent a genocide."
Richard Holbrooke, U.S. diplomat

"We fought this conflict because . . . we believed it was wrong to have ethnic cleansing and racial genocide here in Europe toward the end of the 20th century."
Tony Blair, British Prime Minister

KOSOVO

Control of Kosovo, a province of Serbia, was disputed between Serbs and Albanians for centuries. In the 1970s and 1980s, Kosovo was quite independent of Serbia, with Serbian and Albanian Kosovans living together. But in 1989, Serbian nationalists under Slobodan Milosevic ended Kosovo's independence and discriminated against the majority Albanian population. In the mid-1990s, some Albanian Kosovans formed the UCK (in English, the Kosovo Liberation Army) and began guerilla warfare against the Serbian police. Serbian politicians responded with extreme force, causing civilian casualties in Albanian areas and creating tens of thousands of refugees.

After U.S.-sponsored peace talks failed, NATO intervened in March 1999, without UN approval. The NATO action was confined to bombing from aircraft. More than a million Kosovans fled the bombing and the Serbian militias on the ground. NATO also bombed cities in Serbia to force Milosevic to admit defeat. When he did so, NATO troops moved into Kosovo. Kosovo is now run by the UN, with limited democracy. Most Albanian Kosovan refugees have returned, but roughly 200,000 Serbian Kosovans fled the province.

MORE TO THINK ABOUT

Ramush Haradinaj was a UCK leader who became Kosovan prime minister. In 2005, he was charged with war crimes. Would NATO's case for war be harmed if those NATO helped were war criminals?

NO "I think the bombing did cause the ethnic cleansing. ... NATO's action in Kosovo was mistaken. ... What we did made things much worse."
Lord Carrington, NATO's former Secretary General

✖ "NATO's actions are equally criminal with those of Milosevic."
Nelson Mandela, former President of South Africa

✖ "The [NATO] aggressors have tossed the UN aside and begun a new era, when the strong bear down and dictate their will. ... It was such good luck the Serbs are a defenseless target."
Alexander Solzhenitsyn, "Solzhenitsyn Compares NATO, Hitler," in The Moscow Times

✳ STATISTICALLY SPEAKING

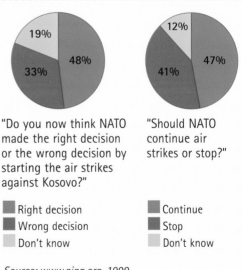

"Do you now think NATO made the right decision or the wrong decision by starting the air strikes against Kosovo?"

- Right decision
- Wrong decision
- Don't know

"Should NATO continue air strikes or stop?"

- Continue
- Stop
- Don't know

Source: www.pipa.org, 1999

FIND OUT MORE: www.nato.int www.counterpunch.org/biglie.html
www.iwpr.net www.globalissues.org/Geopolitics/Kosovo.asp

25

Q: Does terrorism ever make sense?

TERRORISM IS the threat and use of violence to achieve a political goal. Terrorism is used by groups who think they are failing to achieve their goals by peaceful persuasion. It may also be used by whole communities resisting a well-armed occupying force. In both cases, terrorism serves two main purposes—it harms the group's enemies, and it gives the group itself a sense of purpose. But terrorism may often not be capable of bringing about the group's political goals.

YES

"Violence spreads fear and panic and gives us a place in the scheme of things."

Unnamed leader of the Pakistani terror group Lashkar-e-Jhangvi, in The Atlantic

"In 1974, [Palestine Liberation Organization (PLO)] leader Yasser Arafat was invited to speak at the United Nations General Assembly shortly after a string of deadly Palestinian attacks on airlines and Israeli civilians, including children."

Suzy Hansen, talking about the terrorist group the PLO, which was originally committed to the creation of a separate Palestinian state but in 1993 pledged peaceful coexistence with Israel

NO

"Some of my colleagues say [Islamist terrorist group] Al Qaeda is all about a political objective, and that objective is to force [the U.S.] out of Saudi Arabia. They see [leader] bin Laden and Al Qaeda as rational in the sense of having a rational goal and going after it in the most cost-effective way they can. I don't think that's really true. . . . Their [claimed] objective changes regularly."

Jessica Eve Stern, interviewed at reason.com

"The fact we are gathered here, now, shocked but composed and determined, is a sign not only that this attack has failed, but that all attempts to destroy democracy by terrorism will fail."

Margaret Thatcher, former U.K. prime minister, after surviving a terrorist bomb

"We all know that terrorism is wrong, and we all rightly condemn it. . . . What relationships do Muslims and indeed any faith community have with terrorism? The answer is NOTHING."

Dr. Fiaz Hussain, spokesperson for the Luton Council of Mosques, U.K.

Nelson Mandela (opposite, right) attends an official ceremony to mark the beginning of his presidency of South Africa in 1994.

CASE STUDY

SOUTH AFRICA

In 1948, the National Party of South Africa brought in apartheid—a discriminatory policy against the black majority of the country. It involved segregation of black and white people in everything, including social interaction, marriage, work, and education.

Nelson Mandela was the organizer of the African National Congress's (ANC) terror wing, Umkhonto we Sizwe (Spear of the Nation). He formed it in 1960 in response to the regime's shootings of black protesters in massacres such as the one at Sharpeville in March 1960.

After his imprisonment in 1962, Mandela issued a famous statement to South Africans: "Those who live by the gun shall perish by the gun. Unite! Mobilize! Fight on! Between the anvil of united mass action and the hammer of the armed struggle, we shall crush apartheid!" Spear of the Nation maintained its campaign of violence into the 1980s. The South African government offered to release Mandela in 1985 if he would publicly abandon armed struggle. He refused, remaining in prison until 1990. Apartheid was abolished in South Africa in 1993. Mandela was elected president of South Africa in 1994 in the country's first multiracial elections.

✿ STATISTICALLY SPEAKING

Terrorism deaths by target, 1990–2005	
Abortion-related	2
Military	428
Police	2,014
Private citizens	4,878
Religious figures	1,207
Tourists	501

Source: www.tkb.org

MORE TO THINK ABOUT

Terrorism is offensive to democratic ideals. Yet some terrorists (such as Nelson Mandela) come to be seen as freedom fighters or heroes if they are seen to have fought for democracy. Do some political "ends" justify the use of terrorist "means" for you?

FIND OUT MORE: www.tkb.org www.osce.org/atu
www.un.org/Docs/sc/committees/1373 www.ict.org.il

Q: Should Amnesty International support attacks on "rogue" regimes?

AMNESTY INTERNATIONAL (AI) is the world's leading campaign group for defending human rights globally. It puts pressure on governments that undermine human rights, alerting the media and its network of activists to human rights abuses. For example, it organizes international letter-writing campaigns to show support for political prisoners. Human rights are becoming a popular reason for military action in Western nations. Amnesty International might support such interventions but would run the risk of being seen as a tool of Western "imperialism."

Amnesty U.K. members vote on a 2005 motion that states: "that AI's default position should be to remain strictly neutral on decisions . . . to deploy or use military force. However, in exceptional circumstances, Amnesty International should reserve the option of reluctantly calling for . . . armed intervention for the purposes of human protection." The proposal was outvoted.

THE INTERNATIONAL COMMITTEE OF THE RED CROSS

The ICRC is an organization that ensures protection and assistance for victims of war and violence. It insists on taking a neutral stance in any conflict. But its emphasis on neutrality is sometimes criticized as a way of avoiding taking a moral stand. The ICRC says: "Neutrality means making no judgment about the merits of one person's need as against another's; it does not mean condoning violations of international humanitarian law."

YES "International responsibility for the universal protection of human rights has gained wider acceptance. . . . Many individual AI members believe that armed intervention is the logical next step in this process and that there are circumstances in which soldiers should be deployed to prevent or end human rights violations."

Pierre Sané, AI Secretary General

"The sad reality is that when all the attempts at persuasion have failed, only force can succeed. . . . We are in front of a tragedy [in Kosovo] in which neutrality is inhumane, in which the military and the humanitarians have no other solution than marching together. Terrible paradox!"

Jose Gramunt, commentary in Presencia, *a Catholic magazine*

"We were slightly constrained by the fact that our mandate does not allow us to call for international intervention."

Carina Tertsakian, AI spokesperson

NO "When people ask me, 'How can we remove unpopular regimes?' I answer, 'It is not up to us to do it. It has to come from the people. Change has to be organic. Imperial interventions never work."

Tariq Ali, antiwar activist

"If [a people] have not sufficient love of liberty to be able to [win] it from merely domestic oppressors, the liberty which is bestowed on them by other hands than their own will have nothing real, nothing permanent. No people ever was and remained free, [except when] it was determined to be so."

John Stuart Mill, "A Few Words on Nonintervention" (1859)

"Concern for the life, safety, and security of the Iraqi people is sorely missing from the debate, as is any discussion on what would be their fate in the aftermath of conflict."

Irene Khan, Amnesty International Secretary General, "Human Rights in the Balance"

MORE TO THINK ABOUT

Remaining impartial helps to protect an international organization from making enemies of certain populations. But it carries the cost of having to stand aside when intervention might urgently be needed. Human Rights Watch (www.hrw.org) calls for intervention. Should Amnesty International join it?

Q: Is ethnic hatred the world's biggest threat to peace?

MANY OF the civil wars and crises that the UN has become involved in since the end of the Cold War have been between ethnic groups within a nation. It is normal (and simple) to explain such conflicts as examples of "ethnic hatred." But to what extent is ethnic hatred an explanation? Do people hate each other simply for being different or for other, deeper reasons, such as perceptions of injustice?

CASE STUDY

KURDISTAN

Kurdistan is a mountainous region in the Middle East. The 20 to 25 million Kurds who live there are the largest ethnic group in the world without their own nation. Throughout their history, they have been ruled by various conquerors and nations. Since the early 20th century, the region has been divided between Turkey, Iran, Syria, and Iraq, all of which have repressed—often brutally—their Kurdish minority.

The HPG is a violent group, linked to the Kurdistan Workers Party (PKK), which fought against Turkey to create an independent homeland for the Kurdish people throughout the 1980s and 1990s. Its attacks against Turks could be understood as "ethnic hatred" for Turks by Kurds. At times, the HPG claimed it was working toward socialist revolution. But it makes more sense to understand the group's violence as due to nationalism—the desire for an independent nation.

"Freedom fighters," or "terrorists," of the Kurdistan Workers' Party train for combat in 1991.

YES

"The . . . conflicts in Yugoslavia, Northern Ireland, and the Middle East are testaments to the terrible durability of ethnic hatred. It is proper and possible to protect ourselves by eliminating individuals and depriving terrorist groups of resources and sanctuary, but our acts will assuredly spawn a new group of fanatics."

Michael Josephson, founder of the Joseph & Edna Josephson Institute of Ethics

"The role of [ethnic] militias in the Sierra Leone civil war shows that they only worsen conflicts."

Editorial, Gambia's Daily Observer

"The disturbing reality is that global markets . . . have intensified the extraordinary economic dominance of certain 'outsider' minorities, fueling virulent ethnic envy and hatred among the impoverished majorities around them."

Professor Amy Chua, Yale University

✿ STATISTICALLY SPEAKING

Nationalist / ethnic conflicts settled more frequently since Cold War

Year	Conflicts starting	Conflicts settled
1945–49	16	5
1950–54	0	7
1955–59	5	1
1960–64	9	3
1965–69	7	0
1970–74	1	6
1975–79	8	1
1980–84	8	2
1985–89	8	5
1990–96	14	20

Source: Bill Ayres, "A World Flying Apart?" Journal of Peace Research

NO

"I [examined] civil conflict since 1965, expecting to find a close relationship between measures of [ethnic] hatreds and grievances and the incidence of conflict. Instead, I found that economics appears to be central to understanding why civil wars get going. Conflicts are far more likely to be caused by economic opportunities than by grievance."

Paul Collier, "Doing Well out of War," World Bank conference paper

"Living in a bad neighborhood, with undemocratic neighbors or neighbors at war, significantly increases a country's risk of experiencing ethnic civil war."

Nicholas Sambanis, "Do Ethnic and Non-Ethnic Civil Wars Have the Same Causes?"

"Ethnic differences are not given in nature; ethnicity does not arise suddenly and spontaneously, but only in specific historical circumstances. . . . It is unlikely to become a lethal force in human affairs except through the deliberate calculation of political elites."

David Turton (ed.), War and Ethnicity: Global Connections and Local Violence

MORE TO THINK ABOUT

How important is your ethnicity to you? Do you feel loyalties to others in your ethnic group? Would you be prepared to kill for them? Try to imagine a situation that would make you do so. Would it be your ethnicity or the situation itself that really explains your actions?

FIND OUT MORE: www.providence.edu/polisci/students/genocide/home.html
www.thecommonwealth.org www.preventgenocide.org

Q: Does the UN act independently of U.S. interests?

THE UNITED Nations was set up by the U.S. in New York City. The U.S. has the final say at the International Monetary Fund (IMF) and the World Bank. The U.S. also has the world's most powerful economy, and its armed forces outspend the combined forces of the EU. In all of these ways, it is able to influence the decisions the UN makes. But the UN is usually seen as independent, in spite of these challenges.

✸ STATISTICALLY SPEAKING

U.S. spending on UN peacekeeping, in context:
• During the past decade, the U.S. spent more than $30 billion on unilateral or U.S.-led military interventions overseas, including operations in Iraq, Bosnia, and Kosovo.
• The U.S. spends more than $50 billion per year deploying more than 260,000 troops and their weapons overseas.
• The $500 million that the U.S. spends in a year on [UN peacekeeping] in 15 regions around the world is only one-fourth of what it spends to purchase one B-2 bomber.

Source: Friends Committee on National Legislation

YES

"The UN is not playing handmaiden to the U.S.... [It] is an association of member states. On many issues, other members naturally look to the U.S. for leadership."
Dysane Dorani, UN information director, interviewed in The Cairo Al-Ahram

✓ "Europeans collectively give 3 times more development assistance to poor countries than the U.S. and provide 10 times the number of peacekeepers to UN operations. Indeed, it is Europe's well-trained peacekeepers that the U.S. now needs in Iraq to keep the lid on the insurgency."
Parag Khanna, "U.S. Could Learn from EU"

✓ "[This report] finds the United States routinely outmatched and outsmarted in the UN by a small but skillful group of repressive regimes.... [It criticizes] U.S. practices at the UN that it says undermine Washington's effectiveness, including:
• U.S. reluctance to support international agreements
• the practice of withholding or threatening to withhold dues
• long-term gaps in the confirmation of a U.S. permanent representative to the UN."
David Dreier & Lee Hamilton, "Enhancing U.S. Leadership at the UN"

✸ STATISTICALLY SPEAKING

• Number of wars the UN has authorized since 1948: two (Korean War—1950, Gulf War—1991).

NO

"As everybody knows, the UN moves only if the United States moves, and the United States—as explicitly indicated by Defense Secretary William Cohen—has no intention, whatsoever, of moving."

Cesare de Carlo, discussing East Timor

"If I were redoing the Security Council today, I'd have one permanent member because that's the real reflection of the distribution of power in the world: . . . the United States."

John Bolton, American diplomat

"Why should Israel be above the law? Because some members of the Security Council—or one member [i.e., U.S.], maybe—is all the time protecting Israel. If the UN is to be fair, there should not be double standards."

Yahya Mahmassani, League of Arab States spokesperson

MORE TO THINK ABOUT

U.S. armed forces account for 45 percent of the world's military spending—more than the EU, Russia, China, and Japan put together. Should the UN's decision-making process reflect this inequality, or should it act as if all members are equal?

The UN needs the military resources of its members to enforce its decisions. Only the U.S. can afford resources such as this $2.1 billion B-2 "stealth" bomber.

FIND OUT MORE: www.peacecorps.gov   www.lowyinstitute.org
www.un.org/Docs/sc   www.getusout.org

Q: Will environmental crises lead to wars?

As THE world's climate and geography evolve over time, some places become impossible to farm or lose water and other vital resources. Others become more valuable. These natural processes are normally so gradual that people's lifestyles gently adapt. But many scientists are warning that global warming will cause many more dramatic changes. Rising sea levels may force people in lowland countries to find new spaces to live, fish, and farm. They may have to fight for precious natural resources, especially water. Is the best way to keep peace in the world to take action on the environment?

CONFLICTING EVIDENCE?

"The world is already full, and the population is too large for the soil."

St. Jerome, (A.D. 383—global population: 250 million).
Source: "The Myth of Famine," www.catholiceducation.org

"Resources are not fixed and finite because they are not natural. They are a product of human ingenuity, resulting from the creation of technology and science."

Source: Thomas De Gregori, "Resources Are Not; They Become," in Journal of Economic Issues (September 1987)

NO "I think, at the moment at least, the tendency [in water resource disputes] is still toward cooperation at the international level."

Eva Ludi, in "Swisspeace Strives to Prevent Water Wars"

✖ "Passing the threshold of violence definitely depends on sociopolitical factors and not on the degree of environmental degradation as such."

Günther Baechler, "Why Environmental Transformation Causes Violence"

✖ "Environmental problems can have a serious and long-lasting negative influence on people's living conditions and can lead to economic and social problems, such as poverty, food insecurity, poor health conditions, and migration, within, as well as between, countries. Even so, they seldom directly cause or trigger crisis and conflict."

Kurt Lietzmann & Gary Vest, "Environment and Security," for NATO

LESOTHO

"In September [1998], a massive World Bank-funded water project in the African nation of Lesotho helped spark precisely the type of armed confrontation water experts predict. South African troops invaded Lesotho 'to quell public protests against the lack of democratic reforms.' But newspapers in the region reported that protection of the South African-built Lesotho Highlands Water Project—which pipes water from Lesotho into South Africa's dry industrial heartland—was a major military priority. What has been called the region's 'first water war' left 17 people dead near one of the project's dams, and dozens more in and around the capital."

Source: Korinna Horta & Lori Pottinger, "U.S. Can Help Stop Brewing Water Wars"

The Katse Dam, one of several in Lesotho, creates a water resource worth fighting over.

YES

"Fierce national competition over water resources has prompted fears that water issues contain the seeds of violent conflict."

Kofi Annan, UN Secretary-General

✓ "International disputes arise especially between nations mutually dependent upon the cooperative use of international river basins. Although the cases examined . . . did not result in violent clashes, considerable potential for military actions persists."

Günther Baechler, "Why Environmental Transformation Causes Violence"

✴ STATISTICALLY SPEAKING

Of 40 cases of severe environmental disputes:

2	were resolved by bureaucratic methods
9	caused political tension or military threats
11	resulted in minor violent incidents but no sustained violent conflict
10	resulted in violent conflict
8	involved wars

Source: Environmental Conflicts Project (ENCOP)

MORE TO THINK ABOUT

Disputes over control of economic resources—such as oil, timber, or diamonds—are more common than wars due to environmental changes. Do you think nature will have more or less impact on human society in the future?

FIND OUT MORE: www.ecr.gov www.cato.org/research/nat-studies/population.html
www.unfccc.int www.swisspeace.org

Q: Should alleged human rights criminals be tried in an international court?

COUNTRIES NEED independent courts to prevent powerful people from perverting justice. But even courts work within laws made by politicians and the voters they represent. This makes it difficult to establish a court at an international level—there are no international elections, for example. In 2002, an International Criminal Court (ICC) was established by 66 countries, against protests from China, Iraq, Israel, Libya, Qatar, the U.S., and Yemen. America demanded that supporters of the ICC not use it to prosecute U.S. citizens. Those who resisted U.S. demands risked losing American aid money.

CHILE'S DICTATOR

General Augusto Pinochet was dictator of Chile from 1973 to 1990. He staged a coup against a socialist government and exterminated his political opponents. Approximately 3,000 were murdered, many dumped into the Pacific Ocean from "Caravan of Death" helicopters. In the late 1990s, there were various attempts by European countries to bring him to justice, although nothing eventually happened. Spanish judge Baltasar Garzón issued a warrant for Pinochet's arrest in 1998, as the ex-dictator relaxed in the U.K. Pinochet was excused from prosecution on "health" grounds in 2000, but Chilean judges began to act. Pinochet was extradited to Chile and faced prosecution there. But Pinochet's last act as dictator had been a change to Chile's laws, making it almost impossible to prosecute him. International laws are much harder for a head of state to undermine.

General Augusto Pinochet (left) stands next to President Salvador Allende, the man who Pinochet staged a coup against in 1973.

SOUTH AMERICA

PACIFIC OCEAN

CHILE

ATLANTIC OCEAN

YES "The ICC ends the impunity of dictators who could kill thousands but not be held to account because they controlled their domestic courts. At the time, I welcomed its creation as putting the Pol Pots [a former Cambodian leader] of the future on notice."

Robin Cook, former U.K. Secretary of State for defense

"[In the ICC] lies the promise of universal justice. [Nations should do their part] to ensure that no ruler, no state, no junta, and no army anywhere can abuse human rights with impunity."

Kofi Annan, UN Secretary-General

"The ICC will have a deterrent effect. It will send a clear message that the international community will not tolerate these crimes, and the full weight of the law will be brought to bear on perpetrators."

Amnesty International

NO "I wouldn't join the International Criminal Court. It's a body based in The Hague, where unaccountable judges and prosecutors can pull our troops or diplomats up for trial."

George W. Bush, U.S. President

"The activities of the Court should not run counter to the provisions of the Charter of the United Nations."

Chinese Ministry of Foreign Affairs Web site

"No U.S. citizen is going to be tried by a Belgian."

Unidentified U.S. State Department official

✳ STATISTICALLY SPEAKING

Americans prefer ICC

Q: Do you think it would be better to refer (Darfur war criminals) to:

The International Criminal Court	60%
A Temporary tribunal	29%

Source: Chicago Council on Foreign Relations survey (March 1, 2005)

ICC full members, February 2005

Region	Number of full members	Number agreeing to immunity for U.S. citizens & employees	Number losing U.S. aid after refusing immunity
Africa	27	20	8
Asia	12	5	-
Eastern Europe	15	6	2
Latin America & Caribbean	19	8	10
Western Europe & other	25	3	2
TOTAL	98	42	22

Sources: www.iccnow.org, www.amicc.org

MORE TO THINK ABOUT

The International Criminal Court tries people for breaking international laws. Could international laws conflict with the laws chosen by citizens within a nation? Which should take priority?

FIND OUT MORE: www.iccnow.org www.benferencz.org www.icc-cpi.int www.amicc.org

Q: Can the Palestinian-Israeli conflict be solved by peace talks?

IN 1948, a new state called Israel was created in the areas of Palestine under Jewish control. Palestinian Arabs in the area had to accept being ruled by a Jewish state, or leave. Many gathered in the Gaza Strip and the West Bank, including part of Jerusalem. Bitter fights broke out between some of these Arabs and the Israeli security forces. Palestinian armed rebellions, or intifada, occurred from 1987 to 1991, and again in 2000. Widespread civilian casualties and bitterness on both sides have made peace very hard to achieve.

Israel was born after World War II, out of territory previously run by colonial powers.

YES "The real [hope] is to say that with all the power of our [Israel's] army—and we have awesome power—we knew when to say no [to armed conflict]."

David Zonsheine, spokesperson for Courage to Refuse

"What remains baffling is that topics that are off-limits for discussion in the United States get a much fuller hearing in Israel itself. Compare the diversity of critical opinions that appear in Israel's major newspapers to those in the United States—you'd think the United States has a greater stake in defending the occupation than does Israel."

Shamil Idriss, "Mideast Peace Won't Come by Sweeping Conflict Aside"

"I can never take the word Israel off my passport, or the word Arab, which I feel proud of. . . . We don't have to be caught [between the two]; we can lead these two worlds and still keep everything we had."

Asel Asleh, Seeds of Peace graduate

✿ STATISTICALLY SPEAKING

• Division of the territory between Arabs and Jews has been talked about for more than 85 years:

Balfour Declaration 1917
Peel Commission 1936
UN Partition Plan 1947
Madrid Conference 1991
Oslo Peace Accords 1993
Camp David Summit 2000
Road Map for Peace 2002
Sharon Disengagement Plan 2004

PEACE TALKS IN OSLO

In 1993, Norway brought Israeli and Palestinian leaders together secretly in Oslo to talk about a peace deal. Israel agreed to allow the creation of a Palestinian Authority, while the Palestine Liberation Organization promised to abandon violence and become a peaceful political movement. But Yitzhak Rabin, the Israeli leader, was assassinated in 1995, and peace failed.

(Left to right) Shimon Peres, Yitzhak Rabin, and Yasser Arafat accept Nobel Peace Prizes in December 1994.

✿ STATISTICALLY SPEAKING

Israelis

| Favor a Palestinian state based on 1967 borders, if Palestinians commit to stop using violence. | 51% | 21% | Oppose, because Israel must continue to hold territories. |
| | | 19% | Oppose, because do not believe Palestinians will stop. |

Palestinians

| Favor stopping violence if Israelis agree to state based on 1967 borders and negotiate other issues. | 42% | 30% | Oppose, because favor struggle for all of historic Palestine. |
| | | 18% | Oppose, because do not believe Israel will agree to 1967 borders. |

Source: www.sfcg.org

NO

"There is no solution to the conflict in this region except with the disappearance of Israel. Peace settlements will not change reality, which is that Israel is the enemy and that it will never be a neighbor or a nation. Peace will not wipe out the memory of the massacres it has committed."

Sheikh Hassan Nasrallah, Hizbollah leader, speech in Beirut

✗ "This agreement [Oslo], I am not considering it more than the agreement that had been signed between our prophet Muhammad and Quraish."

Yasser Arafat, former Palestinian leader, comparing Oslo Accords to a false pact the Prophet Muhammad made in order to weaken his enemy

✗ "More than two of every three Americans (68 percent) agree that it is reasonable for the Israeli government to insist on an end to suicide bombings and other acts of terrorism before making concessions to the Palestinians."

Travis Clark, reporting survey findings

MORE TO THINK ABOUT

The conflict between Israel and the Palestinians was a source of international terrorism for 30 years. Do you think solving that conflict will convince terrorists to return to peaceful politics?

Q: Will laws against land mines work?

LAND MINES ARE small, hidden bombs that explode when a person or vehicle touches their trigger mechanism. In warfare, they serve the task of "area denial"—making a piece of land unusable for enemy troops. Armies planting mines are supposed to keep detailed records about where they are hidden so that they can be removed safely when the war is over. But mines often stay hidden after the war has ended, wounding hundreds of civilians and precious farm animals each year. Civilians cannot live in peace even when the war is over. This has led to calls for land mines' complete ban.

A young boy at an Angolan rehabilitation center for mine victims. Many people were displaced by the civil war, and areas were heavily mined.

YES

"The progress made since the Mine Ban Treaty entered into force five years ago is a great example of what governments can achieve when they work cooperatively to increase human security under a multilateral process."

Deborah Morris-Travers, Campaign Against Land Mines, New Zealand

"Antipersonnel mines still kill and maim innocent people every day. . . . Anti-vehicle mines pose a grave threat, too. We cannot rest until all land mines are cleared and these indiscriminate weapons banished forever."

Kofi Annan, UN Secretary-General, at the Nairobi Land Mines Conference

"The marked drop in the use of antipersonnel mines around the globe since the mid-1990s is without question one of the great achievements of the Mine Ban Treaty and the movement to ban antipersonnel mines more generally."

Land Mine Monitor Report

✻ STATISTICALLY SPEAKING

• In 2002, more than 11,700 new land mine casualties were identified, including 2,649 children (23 percent) and 192 women (2 percent). Less than 15 percent were military personnel.

Sources: www.americanprogress.org, Tommy Franks, Lancet

NO "A lot of arms-producing companies in Europe are still involved in the development, production, and export of land mine-related technologies. And even the small budgets for humanitarian de-mining . . . are used in part to finance [the mine-detection technology] projects of mine-producing companies."

Actiongroup Land Mine, Germany

✗ "Forty-two countries, with a combined stockpile of some 180 to 185 million antipersonnel mines, remain outside of the Mine Ban Treaty. They include three of the five permanent members of the UN Security Council (China, Russia, and the U.S.)."

Land-Mine Monitor Report

✗ "The call for a mines' ban is unworkable, undesirable, and, worse, counterproductive. The campaign diverts attention and funds from the real issue. It enables governments to claim that they are spending money on dealing with the problem of land mines, whereas, in fact, they are spending money on discussing the problem, on hosting conferences, on carrying out 'assessment missions,' on promoting 'mine awareness' campaigns—on almost everything, in fact, other than the messy business of actually getting the mines out of the ground."

Paul Jefferson, mine clearer, "Why Diana Is Wrong"

CASE STUDY

CLUSTER BOMBS

Area denial may be achieved by dropping "cluster bombs" from the air. Each bomb breaks open to scatter hundreds of bomblets across an area. Most explode, but around five percent survive, to threaten anything that moves near them. In October 2001, UN land mine experts appealed to the U.S. to identify the type of cluster bomb it had dropped around Shaker Qala, a village in Afghanistan. The bomblets were trapping villagers in their houses, and UN land mine experts did not know how to make them safe.

CONFLICTING EVIDENCE?

Australia destroyed its operational stocks of approximately 135,000 land mines shortly after ratification in 1999.

Source: Alexander Downer, Foreign Minister of Australia

In April 2004, Australia listed 7,465 antipersonnel mines retained for training purposes.

Source: Australian Article 7 Report, Form D

MORE TO THINK ABOUT

It can be hard to define what an antipersonnel weapon is. Should they be defined by the purpose they are designed and built for? Or should they be defined by their possible effect on civilians?

FIND OUT MORE: www.landmines.org www.icbl.org/treaty
www.landmine.de www.calm.org.nz

Q: Is it possible to win a war against terror?

THE FIRST "war on terror" was announced by U.S. President Ronald Reagan in the 1980s. With the end of the Cold War, international terrorism was reduced. But a portion of the Islamic extremists who had fought against the USSR in Afghanistan were committed to carrying on. George W. Bush announced a second "war on terror" in 2001 in response to the terrorist attacks on New York and Washington, D.C. This time, the war was to include U.S. invasions of Afghanistan and Iraq.

YES

"We do not believe that Americans are fighting this evil to minimize it or to manage it. We believe they are fighting to win—to end this evil before it kills again and on a genocidal scale. There is no middle way for Americans: it is victory or holocaust."

Richard Perle & David Frum, An End To Evil: How To Win the War on Terror

"One of the interesting things people ask me, now that we are asking questions, is, 'Can you ever win the "war on terror"?' Of course you can."

President George W. Bush, White House press conference, April 13, 2004

"We can win it. And I believe ultimately we will win. But it's going to require an emphasis not just on security but obviously on tackling other issues too."

Tony Blair, British Prime Minister

CONFLICTING EVIDENCE?

"By the time the U.S. ended direct rule of Iraq . . . in the summer of 2004, only two percent of Arab Iraqis supported the occupation."

Source: "Is the World Safer Now?" a joint investigation in The London Independent

"Compared with just before the war in 2003, 57 percent of Iraqis now say their life is better overall, compared with 19 percent who say it is worse and 23 percent who say it is about the same."

Source: BBC-ARD-NHK poll

STATISTICALLY SPEAKING

• Estimated costs of the "war on terror" in Iraq, as of March 2005:

30,000 Iraqi soldiers killed
18,000–100,000 civilian mortalities
1,511 U.S. troops killed
11,285 U.S. troops wounded
$200 billion expense for U.S. taxpayers
800,000 fewer oil barrels produced per day

THE FIRST WAR ON TERROR

U.S. President Ronald Reagan explained air strikes on Libya in April 1986 as part of his war on international terrorism: "I warned that there should be no place on Earth where terrorists can rest and train and practice their deadly skills. I meant it. I said that we should act with others, if possible, and alone, if necessary, to ensure that terrorists have no sanctuary anywhere."

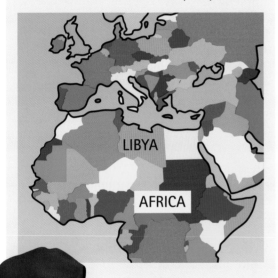

LIBYA

AFRICA

Libya's leader, Colonel Gaddafi, was targeted by the U.S. and U.K. for funding and equipping terrorists who had killed U.S. and U.K. citizens.

NO

"I don't think you can win it. But I think you can create conditions so that those who use terror as a tool are less acceptable in parts of the world."

President George W. Bush, interviewed on NBC's Today show, August 30, 2004

✖ "The CIA probably doesn't have a single truly qualified Arabic-speaking officer of Middle Eastern background who can play a believable Muslim fundamentalist, who would volunteer to spend years of his life with [poor] food and no women in the mountains of Afghanistan. For Christ's sake, most case officers live in the suburbs of Virginia. We don't do that kind of thing."

Anonymous CIA source, to The Atlantic journalist Reuel Marc Gerecht

✿ STATISTICALLY SPEAKING

Total International Terror Attacks 1982–2003

Source: www.sfcg.org

MORE TO THINK ABOUT

The Iraq War occurred too recently for most of us to judge what its long-term effects will be. How do you think it will influence young people—toward democracy or toward religious extremism?

FIND OUT MORE: www.defendamerica.mil www.amnestyusa.org/waronterror/index.do
www.pbs.org/wgbh/pages/frontline/shows/khadr

Glossary

Anarchy "ruled by none"—a society without rules, perhaps resulting in chaos and violence.

Apartheid "separateness"—20th century system of racist government in South Africa.

Apathy lack of interest or energy.

Arms embargo a ban on the sale of weapons to a country.

Autocratic describes rule by one person or group with absolute power.

Belligerents groups in conflict, particularly fighting in a war.

Boycott official or unofficial refusal to trade with a country—for example, refusing to buy its products.

Casualties people wounded or killed by an event, such as a war.

Censorship banning certain types of messages, such as political views or images unsuitable for children.

Citizen a rights-holding member of a nation.

Coalition a temporary group of allies created for a specific task.

Coercive using force, such as military intervention.

Cold War a historical period of rivalry between the U.S. and the USSR (1945–1990).

Consumer a purchaser of goods or services.

Coup (in full: coup d'etat) a sudden change of government illegally or by force.

Credibility trust earned by a person or organization.

Democracy political system in which governments are elected by voters.

Deterioration becoming worse, breaking down.

Deterrent a punishment that acts as a warning to others.

Domestic in international relations, having to do with the home nation of a person or government.

Elites superior groups of people, political leaders, or power holders.

Ethnic cleansing forcing an ethnic group out of a region, usually by terrorizing civilians, or even by murder.

Free speech the right to express any viewpoint without censorship.

Genocide deliberately killing a racial or ethnic group.

Government the group of politicians or other leaders in control of a nation.

Hate speech a political term for expressions that cause offense, implying that speech "is" violence.

Human rights basic rights to life and freedom for everyone, established in UN law.

Humanitarian in support of human survival needs.

Imperialist helping to build or maintain an empire.

Indiscriminate in warfare, unable to select between military targets and innocent civilians.

Jamming blocking broadcast signals, preventing communication.

Journalist a person paid to research, process, or present information in the media.

Justification argument or explanation of the reasons for something.

Mandate powers granted to a person or organization by its governing authority.

Manifesto a public statement of the policies of a political party or government.

Marginalizing making something or someone seem irrelevant and powerless.

Nobel Prize annual award for the world's greatest contribution to science, literature, peace, etc.

Non-governmental organization (NGO) an organization that is independent from the government. Usually, but not always, refers to noncommercial groups.

Occupation control of a region or nation by military forces.

Paramilitary armed and organized like an army, but not officially controlled by a government.

Patronage the support of a powerful person or organization, a "patron."

Policy specific activity or principle recommended by a person or organization.

Political correctness term for sensitive use of language—often overly so—for example, about disabled people.

Preemptive acting to prevent a problem, rather than letting it occur before responding.

Prerequisite something required in advance of another thing, as a foundation for it.

Propaganda biased or misleading stories or arguments designed to win support for a political idea.

Racism hatred of or prejudice against someone because of his or her race.

Rational based on reason, logic, and clear thinking.

Revenue money earned.

Sanctioned punished by exclusion from some international activities.

Sanctuary safe space, beyond the reach of authorities or persecutors.

Sociopolitical having to do with social and political issues, not natural processes.

Superpower nation with the greatest economic and military power.

Tyrant dangerous dictator or ruler.

Unaccountable not subject to democratic influence or control.

Unilateral without allies, acting alone.

Unsustainable only possible for a short period.

Values political or moral instincts, favoring one choice over another.

Veto legal power to overrule a decision that has been made by others.

Vigilante a person who tries to enforce laws without the right to do so, illegally.

Warmonger A person seen as too eager to start wars.

Debating tips

WHAT IS DEBATING?

A debate is a structured argument. Two teams speak, one at a time, for or against a particular issue. Usually, each person is given a time limit, and any remarks from the opposing side are controlled. The subject of the debate is often already decided, so you may find yourself having to support opinions with which you might not agree. You may also have to argue as part of a team, being careful not to contradict what others on your side have said.

After both sides have had their say and have had a chance to answer the opposition, the audience votes for the team it believes has made the best argument.

DEBATING SKILLS

1 Know your subject

Research it as much as you can. The debates in this book give opinions as a starting point, but there are Web sites suggested that offer additional information. Use facts and information to support your points.

2 Make notes

Write down key words and phrases on cards. Try not to read a prepared speech. You might end up losing your way.

3 Watch the time

You may be given a set amount of time for your presentation, so stick to it.

4 Practice how you sound

Try to sound natural. Think about:
Speed—Speak clearly and steadily. Try to talk at a pace that is fast enough to sound intelligent and allows you time to say what you want, but slow enough to be understood.
Tone—Varying the tone of your voice will make you sound interesting.
Volume—Speak at a level at which everyone in the room can comfortably hear you. Shouting does not win debates. Variation of volume (particularly speaking more quietly at certain points) can help you to emphasize important points, but the audience must still be able to hear you.
Don't ramble—Short, clear sentences work well and are easier to understand.

GET INVOLVED—NATIONAL DEBATING LEAGUES

National Forensic League
www.nflonline.org

Debating Matters, UK
www.debatingmatters.com

American Forensic Association
www.americanforensics.org

Alberta Debate and Speech Association
www.compusmart.ab.ca/adebate/

Index

aid 6
Amnesty International (AI)
    28, 29, 37
Annan, Kofi 11, 35, 37, 40
apartheid 10, 27
Arafat, Yasser 26
arms 10, 11, 22, 23
    control of trade in 22, 23

Bosnia 9, 33

Chile 36
China 14
civil wars 5, 7, 18, 19, 24, 25,
    30, 31
Cold War 4, 9, 24, 30, 42
crimes against humanity 14
Croatia 9

democracy 15, 27, 43

East Timor 6, 13, 33
ECOMOG 7
environmental crises 34, 35
ethnic cleansing 24, 25
ethnic hatred 30, 31
European Union (EU) 5, 8, 9,
    32

Gaddafi, Colonel 43
genocide 13, 15, 20, 24
guerrilla warfare 25

human rights 14, 15, 28, 29
Hussein, Saddam 11, 16
Hutu 21

International Committee of
    the Red Cross (ICRC) 6

international community 14,
    15, 20, 21, 24
International Criminal Court
    (ICC) 36, 37
International Monetary Fund
    (IMF) 32
Iraq 12, 13, 16, 19, 28, 29, 33,
    42, 43
Israel 13, 17, 26, 33, 38, 39

Kosovo 5, 9, 15, 19, 24, 25,
    28
Kurdistan 30

land mines 40, 41
Lesotho 35
Liberia 7, 19
Libya 43

Mandela, Nelson 11, 26, 27
military intervention 6, 12
Milosevic, Slobodan 9, 25
Mine Ban Treaty 40, 41

nongovernmental
    organizations (NGOs) 6,
    22
North Atlantic Treaty
    Organization (NATO) 8, 14,
    24, 25

P-5 12, 13
Palestine 26
Palestine Liberation
    Organization (PLO) 39
peacekeeping 12, 18, 19, 20,
    21, 33
peacekeeping forces 4, 7, 18,
    19, 21
Pinochet, Augusto 36

refugees 9, 15, 19, 21, 22, 25
Rwanda 13, 15, 20, 21

sanctions 10, 11, 12
Serbia 24, 25
South Africa 10, 27
sovereignty 14
Srebrenica 19
Sudan 22

terrorism 16, 17, 26, 27, 30
Tiananmen Square 14
Tutsi 20

UNAMIR 20
United Nations (UN) 4, 6, 10,
    11, 12, 13, 14, 18, 22, 24,
    32, 33, 41
United Nations Security
    Council (UNSC) 4, 6, 12,
    13, 19, 32, 33, 41
United Nations territories 15,
    19, 25
UNMIL 19
U.S. 6, 7, 8, 9, 12, 13, 15, 16,
    21, 25, 32, 33, 36, 37, 38,
    39
USSR 4, 24

veto 12, 13

war 9, 18, 22, 24, 25, 30, 31
    on terror 16, 42, 43
    preemptive 16, 17
water 34, 35
World Bank 32, 35
World War I 8
World War II 4

Acknowledgements

Picture credits: © Marie-Anne Ventoura/Amnesty International U.K.: 28. © Ed Kashi/Corbis: 30. © Reuters/Corbis: 36. © David Turnley/Corbis: 10. © Collart Herve/Corbis Sygma: 35. Michel Lipchitz/AP/Empics: 9. ©Stefan Boness/Panos Pictures: cover, 18. Rex Features: 12. Action Press/Rex Features: 22. Sipa Press/Rex Features: 7, 21, 27, 43. Andrew Testa/Rex Features: 24. Mike Kolloffel/Still Pictures: 40. TopFoto: 4, 17. Topfoto/AP: 14, 39. TopFoto/Photri: 33.

Text credits: Page 6: 1 David Gelernter, "There's a Good Reason He Infuriates the Reactionary Left," *The Weekly Standard*, September 13, 2004, Volume 010, Issue 01; 2 U.K. government, *Strategic Defense Review*, 2001; 3 editorial on East Timor, *The Sydney Daily Telegraph*, Australia, September 8, 1999. Page 7: 1 John Quincy Adams, U.S. Secretary of State, 1821 2 Kweku mamuah, Africa, BBC Online "Talking Point:" http://news.bbc.co.uk/1/hi/talking_point/ 422788.stm; 3 Robert E. White: http://www.washingtonpost.com/wp-srv/liveonline/00/world/ white021600.htm (10/11/05). Page 8: 1 Jacques Chirac, quoted in *Gazeta Wiborcza*, Poland, February 25, 2005; 2 Dusko Lopandic, Serbian European Integration Office, 3 Charles A. Kupchan, "The End of The West," *The Atlantic*, November 1, 2002; 4 Tony Blair, speech to the Polish Stock Exchange, 2000; Page 11: Stanley A. Weiss and Zachary Selden, *"Often Worse than Ineffective Sanctions: Don't Love Them or Hate Them, Make Them Work,"* United Nations *Chronicle*, 1 Volume XXXVI, Number 2, 1999; 2 Michel Rossignol, "Sanctions: The Economic Weapon in the New World Order," Library of Parliament, Research Branch, 1993; 3 Kofi Annan, quoted in "Saddam *'Winning Propaganda War'*" March 24, 2000: http://news.bbc.co.uk/1/hi/ world/middle_east/689873.stm (10/11/05); 4 statement of Nelson Mandela at the United Nations, New York, September 24, 1993; 5 David Cortright and George A. Lopez. *The Sanctions Decade: Assessing UN Strategies in the 1990s*. Lynne Rienner Publishers, 2000, 6 Weiss & Selden, "Often Worse than Ineffective," in *UN Chronicle*, No. 2, 1999; Page 12: 1 Richard Holbrooke, speech at the World Bank, Washington, D.C., February 12, 2004; 2 Dysane Dorani, quoted in http://weekly.ahram.org.eg/2003/629/sc6.htm (10/11/05); 3 Senator John Cherry, speech to Australian Parliament, March 19, 2003; Page 13: 1 Joshua Muravchik, quoted in "Enhancing U.S. Leadership at the United Nations," Chair: Lee H. Hamilton, David Dreier, Director: Lee Feinstein, Adrian Karatnycky, Council on Foreign Relations Press, October 2002; 2 Guy Taillerfer, *Le Devoir*, Canada, September 9, 1999; 3 Carroll Andrew Morse, "The UN: The World's Greatest Trade Association," December 20, 2004: http://www.techcentralstation.com/ 122004A.html; Page 15: 1 President Paul Kagame, "Talking Point" Special: Ask Rwanda's President, April 27, 2004: http://212.58.226.30/1/hi/talking_point/3442577.stm; 2 Gary Kamiya, "Smashing the State: The Strange Rise of Libertarianism," *Salon* magazine: http://www.salon.com/jan97/state970120.html (10/11/05); 3 Rein Mullerson, *Human Rights Diplomacy*, Routledge, December 1996; 4 Mahmood Mamdani, "Humanitarian Intervention: A Forum," *The Nation*, July 14, 2003; 5 John T. Correll, "The Doctrine of Intervention," *Air Force Magazine*, February 2000; 6 Jon Holbrook, "In defense of sovereignty," October 2, 2001: http://www.spiked-online.com/Articles/00000002D257.htm (10/11/05); Page 16: 1 George W. Bush, speech to graduates of West Point Military Academy, May 2002; 2 David Horowitz, www.frontpagemagazine.com; Page 17: 1 Senator John Cherry, speech to Australian Parliament, March 19, 2003; 2 Harry S. Truman (1955-56), 3 William F. Schulz, Amnesty International USA, press conference, May 2004; Page 18: 1 Quote cited on: http://www.un.org/News/dh/latest/reasonspage.htm (10/17/05); 2 Page Fortna, "Peace Operations: Futile or Vital?" www.un-globalsecurity.org (Undated); Page 19: 1 Mark Steyn, "UN Forces—Just a Bunch of Thugs?," in *The London Daily Telegraph*, February 15, 2005; 2 Report of the Panel on UN Peace Operations, August 2000; 3 David Chandler, *Bosnia: Faking Democracy After Dayton*, Pluto Press, 1999; Page 20: 1 Linda Melvern, "Humanitarian Intervention and the Case of Rwanda," on www.h-net.org, April 2003; 2 Samantha Powers, correspondence in *The Atlantic*, December 2001; 3 Alan Kuperman, "A Hard Look at Intervention," *Foreign Affairs*, Jan-Feb, 2000; 4 Taylor Seybolt, "Could Genocide Have Been Stopped in Rwanda?" web.mit.edu/ssp, March 17, 1999; 5 Alan Kuperman, *The Limits of Humanitarian Intervention*, Brookings Institution Press, 2001; 6 Quaker Council for European Affairs, www.quaker.org/qcea, May 1999; Page 22: 1 John D. Holum, "Threat Control Through Arms Control," December 1997: http://usinfo.state.gov/products/pubs/archive/armsctrl/pt1.htm (6/27/05); 2 "Who Calls the Shots?" www.caat.org.uk, February 2005; Page 23: 1 Lord Bach, "MoD Has No Difficulty With York Report," *Financial Times*, March 13, 2002; 2 Josie Appleton, "Jack Straw's Global Gun Law," www.spiked-online.com, March 16, 2005; Page 24: 1 Jamie Shea, BBC News Online / BBC World Service, April 20, 1999; 2 George Robertson, *Hansard*, March 25, 1999; 3 Richard Holbrooke, www.academyofdiplomacy.org, February 12, 2004; 4 Tony Blair quoted in "Blair: End Ethnic Hatred," July 31, 1999: http://news.bbc.co.uk/1/hi/uk/ 408602.stm; Page 25: 1 Lord Carrington, cited in "Kosovo: Law & Diplomacy," www.cps.org.uk;

2 Nelson Mandela, cited in "Flying above the Law," *The Times* (London), May 31, 1999; 3 Alexander Solzhenitsyn, "Solzhenitsyn Compares NATO, Hitler," *Moscow Times*, April 29, 1999; Page 26: 1 Unnamed leader of Pakistani terror group, Lashkar-e-Jhangvi, in *The Atlantic*, June 2004; 2 Suzy Hansen, "Dershowitz's Why Terrorism Works," for salon.com, September 12, 2002; 3 Jessica Eve Stern, interviewed at reason.com, August 21, 2003; 4 Margaret Thatcher, www.bbc.co.uk, October 12, 1984; 5 "Terrorism: Wrong in All Communities," Dr. Fiaz Hussain: http://www.bbc.co.uk/threecounties/content/articles/2005/01/ 08/fiaz_hussain_new_year_message_feature.shtml; Page 29: 1 Pierre Sané, AI Secretary General, Introduction to AI's Annual Report 2000; 2 Jose Gramunt, commentary in *Presencia*, April 6, 1999; 3 Carina Tertsakian, July 27, 1997: http://www.udayton.edu/~rwanda/articles/ genocide/questionsanswers.html; 4 Tariq Ali, speech at St. John's Cathedral, New York, October 14, 2003; 5 John Stuart Mill, "A Few Words on Nonintervention," 1859; 6 Irene Khan, "Human Rights in the Balance," September 15, 2002; Page 31: 1 Michael Josephson "What We Should Remember From September 11": http://www.josephsoninstitute.org/speeches-papers/MJ-Terrorism(2)-0901.htm; 2 editorial, "Now Come the Militia," Gambia's *Daily Observer*; 3 Amy Chua, *World On Fire: How Exporting Free Market Democracy Breeds Ethnic Hatred and Global Instability*; 4 Paul Collier, "Doing Well Out of War," World Bank conference paper, April 10, 1999; 5 Nicholas Sambanis, "Do Ethnic and Non-Ethnic Civil Wars Have the Same Causes?" January 24, 2001; 6 David Turton (ed.), *War and Ethnicity: Global Connections and Local Violence*, Boydell Press, 2003; Page 32: 1 Dysane Dorani, interviewed in the *Cairo Al-Ahram*, March 2003; 2 Parag Khanna, "U.S. Could Learn from EU," *Los Angeles Times*, April 30, 2004; 3 Dreier & Hamilton, "Enhancing U.S. Leadership at the UN," www.cfr.org , October 10, 2002; Page 33: 1 Cesare de Carlo, Italy's *La Nazione*, September 9, 1999; 2 John Bolton, cited in "The World According To Bolton," www.nytimes.com, March 9, 2005; 3 Yahya Mahmassani, www.csmonitor.com, September 27, 2002; Page 34: 1 Eva Ludi, in "Swisspeace Strives to Prevent Water Wars," www.swissinfo.org, April 28, 2003; 2 Günther Baechle, "Why Environmental Transformation Causes Violence," wwics.si.edu, Spring 1998; 3 Lietzmann & Vest, "Environment and Security," for NATO, Report No. 232, March 1999; Page 35: 1 Kofi Annan, quoted in "UN Warns of Looming Water Crisis," March 22, 2002: http://news.bbc.co.uk/1/hi/world/1887451.stm (8/18/05); 2 Günther Baechler, "Why Environmental Transformation Causes Violence," wwics.si.edu, Spring 1998; Page 37: 1 Robin Cook, quoted in, "If not in Darfur, Then Where?" *Guardian* (London), February 11, 2005; 2 Kofi Annan, UN Secretary-General, quoted in "Indepth: War Crimes, The International Criminal Court," CBC News Online, July 9, 2004 (06/29/05); 3 Amnesty International, June 1998: http://web.amnesty.org/library/index/engior400181998?open&of=eng-385; 4 George W. Bush, transcript: first presidential debate, September 30, 2004, from Coral Gables, Florida: http://www.washingtonpost.com/wp-srv/politics/debatereferee/debate_0930.html (06/29/05); 5 http://www.fmprc.gov.cn/eng/wjb/zzjg/tyfls/tyfl/2626/2627/t15473.htm; 6 unidentified U.S. State Department official, cited at www.guardian.co.uk, February 11, 2005; Page 38: 1 David Zonsheine, Courage to Refuse, www.couragetorefuse.org , 2004; 2 Shamil Idriss, "Mideast Peace Won't Come by Sweeping Conflict Aside," www.sfcg.org, January 23, 2004; 3 Asel Asleh, "Asleh is Gone," www.salon.com, October 7, 2000; Page 39: 1 Sheikh Hassan Nasrallah, quoted in "Hizbollah Promises Israel a Blood-filled New Year, Iran Calls for Israel's End," December 31, 1999: http://www.unb.ca/web/bruns/9900/issue14/intnews/israel.html; 2 Yasser Arafat, speech in a mosque, South Africa, May 10, 1994; 3 Travis Clark, reporting survey findings, www.defenddemocracy.org, May 23, 2003; Page 40: 1 Deborah Morris-Travers, Campaign Against Land Mines, New Zealand , November 23, 2004; 2 Kofi Annan, UN Secretary-General, at the Nairobi Land Mines Conference, December 23, 2004; 3 Land Mine Monitor Report 2004, www.icbl.org; Page 41: 1 Actiongroup Land Mine, Germany, www.landmine.de; 2 Land Mine Monitor Report 2004, www.icbl.org; 3 Paul Jefferson, quoted in "Why Diana Is Wrong," *The Daily Telegraph* (London), February 8, 1997; Page 42: 1 Perle & Frum, *An End To Evil: How To Win the War on Terror*, Random House, 2003; 2 President George W. Bush, White House press conference, April 13, 2004; 3 Tony Blair, press conference, September 7, 2004; Page 43: 1 President George W. Bush, interviewed on NBC's *Today* show, August 30, 2004; 2 anon. CIA source, reported by Reuel Marc Gerecht in *The Atlantic*, August 2001.